THE WORLD of BTS

THE ULTIMATE **UNOFFICIAL** FAN GUIDE

Written by Catherine Saunders

First published in Great Britain in 2025 by Welbeck Children's Books

Text copyright © Hodder & Stoughton Limited 2025
Illustrations by The Boy Fitz Hammond
All rights reserved.

ISBN: 978 1 8045 3851 7

1 3 5 7 9 10 8 6 4 2

Wren & Rook
An imprint of
Hachette Children's Group
Part of Hodder & Stoughton Limited
Carmelite House
50 Victoria Embankment
London EC4Y 0DZ

The authorised representative in the EEA is Hachette Ireland, 8 Castlecourt
Centre, Castleknock Road, Castleknock, Dublin 15, D15 XTP3, Ireland
(email: info@hbgi.ie)

An Hachette UK Company
www.hachette.co.uk
www.hachettechildrens.co.uk

Printed and bound in Great Britain by Clays Ltd, Elcograf S.p.A.

CONTENTS

INTRODUCTION

TWENTY-FIRST CENTURY POP ICONS

Since 2013, seven-piece South Korean boyband **BTS** have been slowly but surely taking over the world. With their cool, catchy K-pop songs and slick dance routines, they've topped the charts across the globe, broken countless streaming records and **WON MILLIONS OF FANS**. But RM (Kim Nam-joon 김남준), Jin (Kim Seok-jin 김석진), Suga (Min Yoon-gi 민윤기), J-Hope (Jung Ho-seok 정호석), Jimin (Park Ji-min 박지민), V (Kim Tae-hyung 김태형) and Jung Kook (Jeon Jung-kook 전정국) are **SO MUCH MORE THAN POP STARS**. They are talented songwriters and music producers, best friends who always look out for each other, and role models who truly care about their fans and the world they live in. They're funny *and* wise, and they're absolute fashion icons. (We could easily write a whole book on just their **INCREDIBLE HAIRSTYLES!**)

BTS BACK STORY

 ## WHAT IS K-POP?

Korean pop music, or K-pop, is influenced by lots
of different styles, from traditional Korean music to
western pop, hip-hop to dance music, and Latin music
to R&B (rhythm and blues). It became famous in the
1990s and is often performed by 'idol'* groups who
have been carefully selected and trained by record
companies. As well as being fantastic singers, K-pop
stars also need to be **AMAZING DANCERS**.

---

* Idol groups are made up of talented individuals who are trained to be
K-pop stars.

9

BTS have achieved more than any other K-pop group in history, with their chart success and adoring fandom rivalling only the legendary British group The Beatles (maybe ask your parents or grandparents about them!). However, just when it seemed like everything was going *perfectly*, BTS made a shocking announcement. In October 2022, they revealed that they were going on hiatus (temporary break). **NOOOOOOOOOOO!** BTS fans were **DEVASTATED**. What did this mean? Was it just a fancy way of saying they were breaking up?

NO WAY! Actually, BTS had *two* very important reasons for pressing pause on the group. Firstly, after nine years of albums, tours and interviews, they each wanted to take some time out to mature and think about what they really wanted to say. That meant making music as individuals. But they hoped it would make them stronger as a group in the future.

'We'll be better than before.'

Also, in South Korea, every male is required to do military service (join the army) for **AT LEAST EIGHTEEN MONTHS**. Even famous pop stars.* BTS had to obey the law.

BTS certainly had a lot going on, but they *promised* to get back together in 2025. Despite this, many of their most passionate fans, nicknamed **ARMY** (now that's ironic!) were feeling pretty *heartbroken*.

---

* Only a few people are exempt or allowed to do shorter service. South Korean football captain Son Heung-min served for only three weeks so he could lead the national team to victory at the 2018 Asian Games.

They needn't have worried, though, as BTS had BIG PLANS. From solo albums to TV shows, and from **LEGO® SETS** to adventures in an **ALTERNATE UNIVERSE** (yes, really – more about that later), they had been busy creating *plenty* of things before they joined the army. There would even be a few group projects, after all. BTS were determined to keep their beloved fans happy while they were away.

'I'll faithfully serve and come back . . . Please stay healthy and let's meet all again in 2025!'

Suga

LIKE   SUBSCRIBE

PHEW! WHAT A RELIEF! They definitely weren't breaking up and would even still be making music! The BTS-shaped hole in our lives became a *tiny bit* smaller.

That's really great news, but things are about to get **EVEN BETTER**. What if there was a way to, *somehow*, get closer to BTS? To find out *everything* about them, from how they met to who writes their songs? Maybe take a peek inside their world and find out exactly what makes them so awesome? Does that sound like the best idea since Jimin dyed his hair pink? Well then, we've got exactly what you need!

This book will take you on an **AMAZING JOURNEY**, showing you how seven outrageously talented boys from all over South Korea came together to become the biggest (and let's just get it out there straight away, **THE BEST**) pop band on the planet. Find out how it all started, how incredibly hard they worked, how they conquered every major chart in the world and what they like to do when they're not performing. Share the highs and the lows and get to know each member as an individual *and* as part of the group.

Look out for amazing facts and inspiring quotes along the way, plus tricky quiz questions to test just how much you know about your favourite K-pop stars.

SO STAND TO ATTENTION, BTS ARMY, AND LET'S MARCH STRAIGHT INTO THE WORLD OF

BTS!

CHAPTER

1

BEFORE BTS

Nowadays, BTS are such global icons that it's probably hard to imagine what the world was like before they came along. But let's try. Imagine a time when few people outside of Korea had even heard of K-pop, let alone **LOVED** it. Can you do it? To show you what we mean, we'll need to rewind a little . . .

🔍 THE BIRTH OF K-POP

Let's go back to the early 1990s. Most people in Korea were listening to gentle pop and slow romantic ballads (yawn!) until a group called Seo Taiji and Boys decided to shake things up with some big feelings and a bit of rap in their break-up song 'Nan Arayo' ('I Know'). People loved it and wanted more songs like *that*! **K-POP TOOK OFF!**

From then on there was no stopping K-pop, and creating new idol groups became an important business in Korea. Music companies regularly toured the country looking for new talent and holding auditions. They were looking for people with extra-special talents in the following areas:

- ♪ Singing
- ♪ Dancing
- ♪ Acting
- ♪ Visuals (fashion and style)
- ♪ Songwriting
- ♪ Composing music
- ♪ Production (making songs)

Anyone who passed the auditions (and the standards were *super* high) would then be put through intensive K-pop training, which could take **YEARS**.

🔍 K-POPULAR

It might have been hard to break into, but the K-pop industry was booming. However, this type of music was still relatively unknown outside Korea and Japan, apart from a couple of exceptions. The most famous, by far, was **'GANGNAM STYLE'** by Psy. This song went viral (was watched and shared lots on the internet) thanks

to a funny music video that became the first to reach more than **1 BILLION VIEWS ON YOUTUBE**, and it also reached number two in the US Billboard Hot 100 chart. It showed that with the right song, or the right group, the whole world was ready to love K-pop.*
Basically, the world *needed* BTS . . .

---

* In fact, since the late 1990s, people around the world had become more interested in Korean culture, especially movies. This popularity was known as *hallyu* which means Korean Wave.

CHAPTER 2

BECOMING BTS

K-pop was the music scene in Korea, but in 2010, Bang Si-hyuk, head of Big Hit Music, felt that it was all getting a little bit safe and unoriginal. It was time to change things up a little! He wanted to create something different – a hip-hop-inspired idol group where trainees could tell their own unique stories through their music. He was looking for members who could **RAP, SING AND DANCE**, as well as having **AWESOME PERSONALITIES** that fans would relate to.

FACT ALERT!

Bang Si-hyuk thought of the name Bangtan Sonyeondan (BTS) before he'd even formed the group. It means Bulletproof Boy Scouts.

Kim Nam-joon, aka Rap Monster or RM, was the first to join BTS. Aged sixteen, he had already been rapping for three years and was also a talented songwriter. He was scouted (discovered) by Big Hit and then asked to audition. Everyone was impressed with his maturity, his sincerity and his intelligence.

'I started this because I wanted to say something. There was a message inside me and I wanted to spread it as music.'

▶ ● RM   LIKE   SUBSCRIBE

KIM NAM-JOON
(김남준)

DATE OF BIRTH:	12 September 1994
BORN IN:	Goyang, South Korea
JOB:	Rapper, singer, songwriter, producer
FAVOURITE COLOURS	Black, pink and purple
ALTERNATIVE CAREER	Businessman

NICKNAMES: Formerly Runch Randa, then Rap Monster, now RM

LIKES: Collecting toys and figures, good weather, wearing lip balm, ice skating, being taller than the rest of BTS

WORST HABITS: Losing things, being clumsy, snoring

DID YOU KNOW? RM won awards for his poetry when he was a kid, and he has an IQ of 148, which means that he is 'highly gifted'

TWO'S COMPANY

Next to become part of BTS was Min Yoon-gi, or Suga. He entered a rap competition and impressed Big Hit by coming second. He was signed as a rapper and also as a producer. Suga had not only been writing songs for several years but he also had a part-time job in a recording studio before becoming a trainee, so he had lots of technical skills too.

 # FACT ALERT!

Suga's original rap name was Gloss. He later changed it to Suga, inspired by his favourite basketball position — shooting guard — and the fact that he looks so sweet. **Awww.**

 MIN YOON-GI
(민윤기)

DATE OF BIRTH:	9 March 1993
BORN IN:	Daegu, South Korea
JOB:	Rapper, singer, songwriter, producer
FAVOURITE COLOUR	Black
ALTERNATIVE CAREER	Basketball player, firefighter, musician

NICKNAMES: Suga, Gloss, Agust D, Grandpa (because he is wise and likes napping and fixing things)

LIKES: Playing guitar and piano, cooking, mentoring young idols, quiet places, reading comics, hanging out with Holly, a brown toy poodle who lives with Suga's parents

WORST HABITS: Biting his nails, worrying

DID YOU KNOW? Suga always cries when he eats wasabi because it's so spicy, and he also once slept for twenty hours

The third person to join BTS was Jung Ho-seok. He already had a reputation as an amazing street dancer, having won a national dance competition when he was fourteen, but he was a talented rapper too. Full of positivity and energy, he chose a name that told fans exactly what he wanted to bring to them – J-Hope.

'He makes anyone bright when he's with them.'

● Jin about J-Hope   LIKE   SUBSCRIBE

So RM, Suga and J-Hope started their K-pop training with other trainees who didn't make it into the band. They worked hard and Bang Si-hyuk was impressed by their talents, but he started to think that maybe something was missing from the group. Could BTS become even bigger than he had imagined? So he started looking for more people to add to the line-up.

 JUNG HO-SEOK
(정호석)

DATE OF BIRTH:	18 February 1994
BORN IN:	Busan, South Korea
JOB:	Dancer, singer, songwriter, producer
FAVOURITE COLOUR	Green
ALTERNATIVE CAREER	Tennis player, dance teacher

NICKNAMES: J-Hope

LIKES: Listening to music, playing guitar, shopping, tennis, reading, performing

WORST HABITS: Avoiding exercise, being easily scared

DID YOU KNOW? Wrestler-turned-actor John Cena is a big fan of J-Hope

⊙ RIGHT PLACE, RIGHT TIME

The fourth member of BTS originally wanted to be an actor, but when a Big Hit employee noticed him getting **OFF A BUS**, they saw that he had star quality and asked him to audition. Kim Seok-jin, known as Jin, had very little experience of singing and dancing, but his natural talent won him a place as a trainee. His famous good looks might have helped too!

FACT ALERT!

Once, Jin jokingly called himself 'Worldwide Handsome', but fans agreed with him and the nickname has stuck!

◀ ❚❚ ▶ ─────────●──────────

KIM SEOK-JIN
(김석진)

DATE OF BIRTH:	4 December 1992
BORN IN:	Gyeonggi-do, South Korea
JOB:	Singer, songwriter, producer
FAVOURITE COLOURS	Pink and blue
ALTERNATIVE CAREER	Chef, actor

NICKNAMES: Jin, Worldwide Handsome, Granny (because he is the oldest, likes cooking and cleans up after the others)

LIKES: Playing video games, cooking, snowboarding, playing piano and guitar

WORST HABITS: Telling bad jokes, forgetting to eat or sleep when he's gaming

DID YOU KNOW? Jin co-owns a Japanese restaurant in Seoul with his brother, he has also had his own mukbang show in which he eats a lot of food while filming himself, and he used to have two sugar gliders (flying possums) as pets

YOUNGEST MEMBER

Next to join was the youngest member of the group.
Jeon Jung-Kook, nicknamed Jung Kook, was only
thirteen when he auditioned, unsuccessfully, for a
singing talent show. However, he was such a fantastic
singer that several companies were keen to sign him.
Jung Kook chose BTS over everyone else after seeing
RM perform.

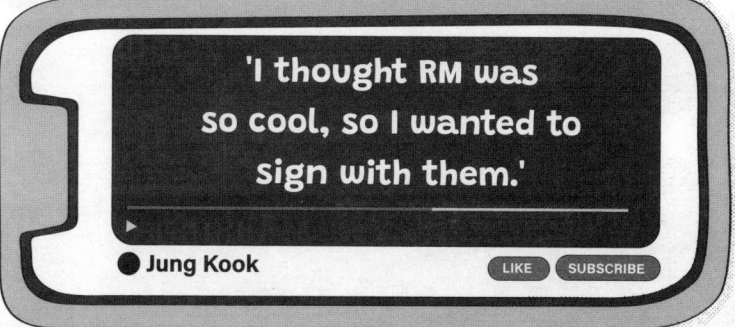

'I thought RM was
so cool, so I wanted to
sign with them.'

● **Jung Kook**   LIKE   SUBSCRIBE

 # FACT ALERT!

The youngest member of a K-pop group is known
as the maknae. Jung Kook is known as the Golden
Maknae because he is just so good at *everything*,
from singing, dancing and rapping to sport.

 ## JEON JUNG-KOOK
(전정국)

DATE OF BIRTH:	1 September 1997
BORN IN:	Busan, South Korea
JOB:	Singer, songwriter, producer, dancer
FAVOURITE COLOURS	Red, black, white and yellow
ALTERNATIVE CAREER	Professional gamer, badminton player

NICKNAMES: Jung Kook, Golden Maknae, Kookie

LIKES: Playing guitar, video games, bowling, football, drawing, buying shoes, reading comic books, cooking, skateboarding

PETS: Bam, a brown Doberman

WORST HABITS: Not eating enough vegetables, not responding to texts, fidgeting

DID YOU KNOW? Jung Kook is a black belt in tae kwon do, and he hates microwaves

ACCIDENTAL STAR

Kim Tae-hyung, or V, nearly didn't audition for BTS at all! He only went along to support a friend but was persuaded to audition too. Unfortunately, his friend didn't make it, and V was the only person picked that day. Awkward . . .

 # FACT ALERT!

V had three choices for his nickname: Lex, Six and V. He chose V because it also stands for victory!

KIM TAE-HYUNG
(김태형)

DATE OF BIRTH:	30 December 1995
BORN IN:	Daegu, South Korea
JOB:	Singer, songwriter, producer, dancer, actor
FAVOURITE COLOURS	Blue, white, green, grey
ALTERNATIVE CAREER	Saxophone player, farmer

NICKNAMES: V, TaeTae

LIKES: Fashion, painting, photography, going to amusement parks

WORST HABITS: Being a picky eater, biting his nails

DID YOU KNOW? V has the deepest voice in the group, he is ambidextrous, which means he can use his right or left hand to do things like write, and V hates wearing shoes

Q BEST FOR LAST?

Park Ji-min, nicknamed Jimin, was cool and confident, and a naturally talented singer, but at first he was only a reserve member of BTS. However, the other six members, especially V, felt that he was the missing piece of their group and insisted that he join the line-up. **BTS WAS COMPLETE!** But they still had a lot to learn . . .

'It was always my dream to perform on stage.'

● RM

LIKE   SUBSCRIBE

PARK JI-MIN
(박지민)

DATE OF BIRTH:	13 October 1995
BORN IN:	Busan, South Korea
JOB:	Singer, songwriter, producer, dancer
FAVOURITE COLOURS	Blue and black
ALTERNATIVE CAREER	Dancer, artist, police officer

NICKNAMES: Jimin, Mochi (after the rice cake with ice cream inside), Chim chim, Little Prince, Dooly

LIKES: Dancing, listening to music, working out, smiling with his eyes

WORST HABITS: Taking ages to get ready, being clumsy

DID YOU KNOW? Jimin practises more than any other member of BTS, he has a black belt in tae kwon do, and wearing eyeliner helps him to feel confident on stage

CHAPTER

3

BUILDING BTS

Some members of BTS spent three years training, while others, such as Jimin, trained for less than a year. K-pop training is **INTENSE** and only the most hard-working and talented trainees make it through. They have to be able to:

- ♪ Sing in perfect harmony
- ♪ Dance in complete synchronisation
- ♪ Perform in front of a huge a crowd
- ♪ Interact with fans positively on social media
- ♪ Become good role models

Alongside this, most trainees also have to finish high school or university! Anyone who doesn't hit K-pop's high standards is sent home and has to do an ordinary job. **GULP**.

TEAM-BUILDING

Training was extra tough for BTS because they also had to perfect their rapping and songwriting. It was a **LOT**, but it was also **EXCITING**. Their K-pop dream was getting closer! The band spent practically every moment with each other, training and practising. They even moved into a tiny apartment together – it had one bedroom with seven bunk beds! Can you *imagine* living with six of your friends? Do you think it would be peaceful and tidy or loud and messy?

 **FACT ALERT!**

RM's snoring often kept the others awake.

For BTS, living and working together was a huge challenge. They were all so different. In the beginning there were some arguments and personality clashes (probably over the washing-up and whose smelly socks had been left on the floor!). But as the boys got to know and care about each other, they started to feel more like a family than a pop group.

'We now know what each of us are thinking just by looking at each other.'

▶

J-Hope

LIKE SUBSCRIBE

Every member of BTS wanted the same thing – **TO BE A K-POP STAR** – and they realised that the best way to achieve that was by working together. So if RM struggled to remember the dance routines, J-Hope could help him. When Jin felt like he wasn't as good at songwriting as the others, RM could guide him. At first, Jung Kook felt shy about performing but Jimin could show him how to look confident. Meanwhile, Jimin didn't think he could rap (he *really* couldn't at first!), but who better than Suga and RM to give him expert tips? And if anyone needed fashion advice, V would always be the ideal person to help.

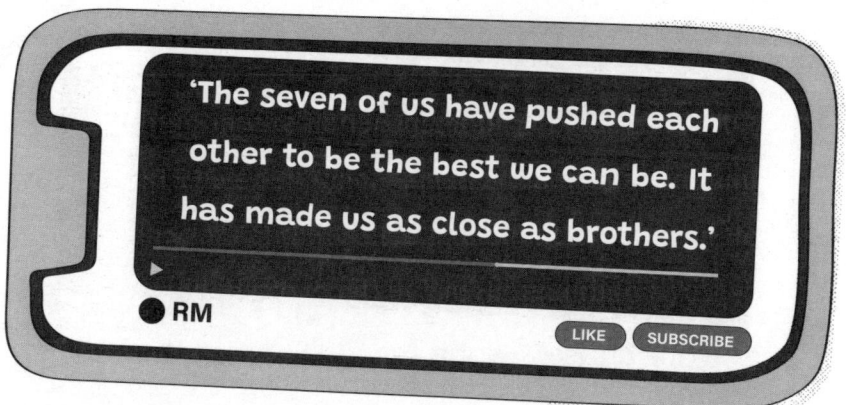

'The seven of us have pushed each other to be the best we can be. It has made us as close as brothers.'

● RM

LIKE SUBSCRIBE

🔍 TEAM LEADER

Friendship, teamwork and understanding each other's talents and differences would become the foundations of BTS's future success. But BTS also needed a leader, someone who would be the group's voice when needed. In Korean culture, the oldest person is usually the most senior, which would have been Jin. However, BTS already had a natural leader, the person who had been in the group the longest – **RM**. Everyone was happy with this choice and RM took his role very seriously. (And that's also why you might find more quotes from RM in this book; he often speaks for the rest of the group, especially in English.)

BTS BACK STORY

Before every performance, BTS do a special handshake
to show that they're ready and that they support each
other. They stand in a circle and each member puts in
the first two fingers on his right hand. Then RM says
'BANG BANGTAN!', the rest answer **'BANGTAN!'**
and then they all move their hands down and away
quickly (never up).

🔍 ARMY ASSEMBLE

You might be thinking that BTS would have been keen to release some music by now, but they still weren't quite ready. One really clever and important part of BTS's K-pop training was all about **BUILDING THEIR FANBASE**. Even before their debut (first performance),

BTS wanted to have some **LOYAL FANS** ready to support them. It would turn out to be a completely brilliant plan!

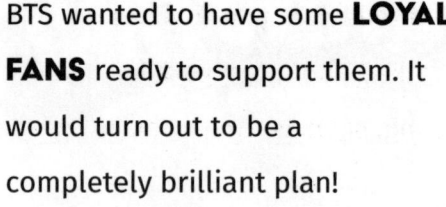

'We had fans who liked us even when we weren't popular.'

LIKE SUBSCRIBE

● Jin

At the end of 2012, more than six months before their debut, BTS started a YouTube channel, **BANGTANTV**. They uploaded videos of themselves practising their moves, addressing their fans, covering other songs or **JUST HAVING FUN**.

It meant that fans could really get to know them, especially when they talked about things that fans might also be feeling, such as Jung Kook's homesickness.

BTS also appeared in music videos and live performances for other K-pop artists, often as back-up dancers. J-Hope even rapped on Jo Kwon's song 'Animal'. It was great practice for them and meant that fans got tantalising glimpses of how **AWESOME** BTS were going to be.

FACT ALERT!

BTS fans soon became known as ARMY, which stands for Adorable Representative MC for Youth.

Social media meant that BTS could connect with their fans, talking to them directly and sharing their personalities and stories. It created a unique and special bond that has only grown stronger over the years. It's not even a slight exaggeration to say that ARMY has been one of the biggest driving forces behind BTS's worldwide success. (ARMY is **DEDICATED AND POWERFUL** – give yourself a big pat on the back right now!)

But let's not jump ahead . . . It was (finally) time for BTS's first ever performance.

Q | THE WAIT IS OVER

So, after years of training, BTS made their official debut. On 12 June 2013, they released their first mini album *2 Cool 4 Skool*, and the next day they performed live on Korean TV. It was only two songs, but they **NAILED IT!** Their dancing and singing were epic and their style and personalities blew fans away. BTS had arrived, but the hard work was just beginning.

FACT ALERT!

Jin had a minor mishap during the
second song on their debut when
his heavy microphone pack made
his trousers fall down! It could have
happened to anyone . . .

BTS BACK STORY

Every year in June, BTS commemorate their debut with
a special fan celebration called BTS Festa. It usually
lasts for several days and includes special videos,
pictures, songs and behind-the-scenes content.

QUIZ: PART ONE

1

What was the name of the K-pop song that was the first video to get more than 1 billion views on YouTube?

A 'HONGDAE STYLE'

B 'ITAEWON STYLE'

C 'GANGNAM STYLE'

2

Who was the first member to join BTS?

A SUGA

B RM

C JIMIN

3 Where was Jin spotted and asked to audition for BTS?

A GETTING OFF A BUS

B AT SCHOOL

C AT THE AIRPORT

4 What does ARMY stand for?

A ALWAYS READY FOR MUSIC AND YOUTUBE

B AMAZING RAP MUSIC YEAH

C ADORABLE REPRESENTATIVE MC FOR YOUTH

5 On which date did BTS make their official debut?

A 14 FEBRUARY 2013

B 1 APRIL 2013

C 12 JUNE 2013

CHAPTER

4

THE EARLY DAYS

BTS's debut was a big success, and not long afterwards they won their first ever award: **BEST NEW ARTIST** at South Korea's Melon Music Awards 2013. Things were going pretty well, but their progress was still **SO MUCH** slower than they had hoped it would be. The phenomenal worldwide stardom that BTS enjoy today didn't happen overnight – it actually took *years* of hard work. And the journey wasn't always smooth . . .

FACT ALERT!

BTS didn't have a number one single
in Korea until 2016!

GOING FOR IT

After spending so long training to be K-pop stars, BTS were used to being patient and knew that there was always room to improve. So they continued to write songs together, practised singing and dancing *even* harder and experimented with different looks. (That must have been so much fun! Do you have a favourite BTS look or is it impossible to pick **JUST ONE?**) They performed live whenever they could, connected with fans via social media and even visited other countries including Japan, the USA and Germany. Day by day, ARMY got **BIGGER** and **MORE PASSIONATE**, gradually spreading the word about BTS online, all around the world.

'We wanted to succeed.'

RM LIKE SUBSCRIBE

BTS BACK STORY

Communicating with fans is so important to BTS that they have developed some signs and symbols which immediately show ARMY that they love them, whether it's in person or via social media. The most important ones are the Korean **FINGER HEART SYMBOL** and the **PURPLE HEART** emoji. (Purple is BTS's signature colour.)

 **GROWING UP**

One of the reasons that the ever-growing ARMY loved BTS was because the boys wrote songs about what was happening to them at that moment and lots of fans were experiencing similar feelings or situations. The group's first three mini-albums, known as the School Trilogy, were themed around **TEENAGE LIFE**, **(GENTLE) REBELLION** and **YOUNG LOVE**. These reflected the things going on in BTS's lives at the time, as many of them were still students as well as pop stars. (Can you imagine having to go to school and be a pop star? When would they even do their homework?)

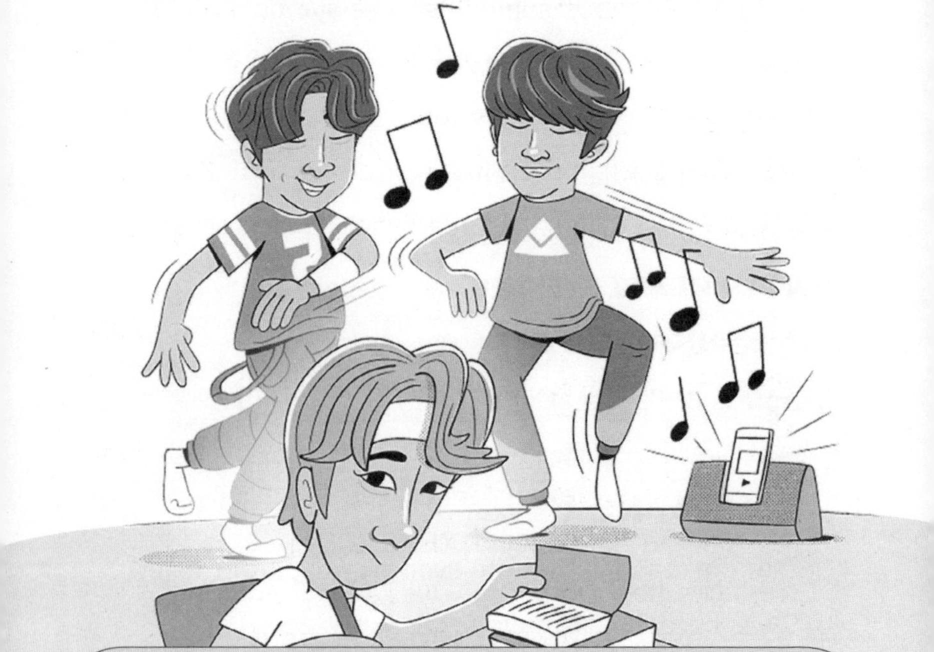

FACT ALERT!

Jung Kook started high school in March 2014, while he was already part of BTS. The rest of the band went with him on his first day and proudly videoed it.

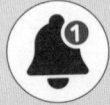

🔍 DARK TIMES

In August 2014, BTS released their first full-length album, *Dark & Wild*. It was one of BTS's darkest albums ever (the clue was in the name, we suppose) and the brooding lead single, 'Danger', was all about problems with love. (It's an *awesome* song with a cool video!) They also set off on their first world tour, **THE RED BULLET TOUR**, which included shows in the USA, Australia and South America, as well as Asia.

 # FACT ALERT!

The largest audience for The Red Bullet Tour was 13,500 people. (By 2021, their audiences would regularly be more than 200,000 people. That's about FOURTEEN TIMES bigger!)

BTS's fan base was growing and they were playing to **BIGGER** and **BIGGER** audiences, but they still didn't really feel like they were reaching the levels they had hoped for. The group began to doubt whether they would *ever* be as popular as they wanted to be, and they were starting to feel burnt out (physically and mentally drained) from working sooooo hard. Pop-star life was **EXHAUSTING** and some people were mean to them online, which was hard to ignore.*

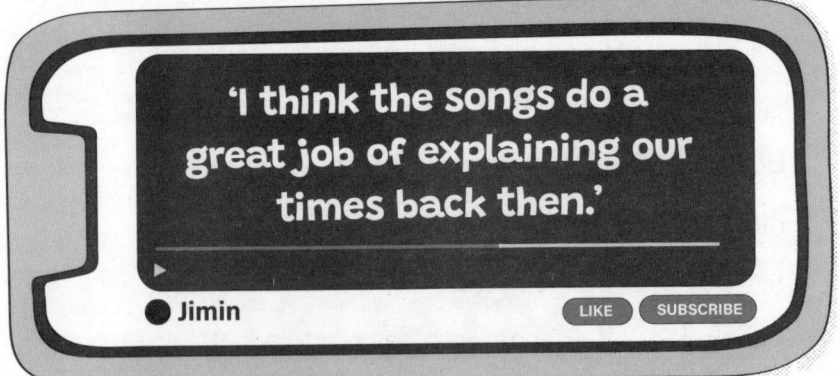

'I think the songs do a great job of explaining our times back then.'

Jimin

LIKE SUBSCRIBE

The boys started to wonder if they were on the right path. Were they making music they really liked? It was a tough time, but they helped each other through it. Their next mini album, *The Most Beautiful Moment in Life Pt. 1* told a very different story. Songs such as 'Dope' reflected the joys and fun parts of growing up. It marked a turning point in BTS's outlook, and also in their popularity.

---

* Posting mean things online is called cyber-bullying and can negatively affect people's mental health.

FACT ALERT!

The video for 'Dope' was BTS's first to get more than 100 million views on YouTube.

RUNNING WITH IT

Keen to give ARMY what they wanted – more BTS – the boys also decided to launch a web series, *Run BTS*, to show their fun and silly sides. In more than 156 episodes, they competed against each other in challenges such as **BUNGEE JUMPING, DRINKING GARLIC JUICE** and **TRAINING DOGS,** or they showed off their acting skills in silly comedy sketches about zombies or school. Sometimes they just played board games or cooked! What really came across was how genuine their friendship is and also how they'll happily betray each other in a heartbeat for the sake of a bowl of ramen noodles!

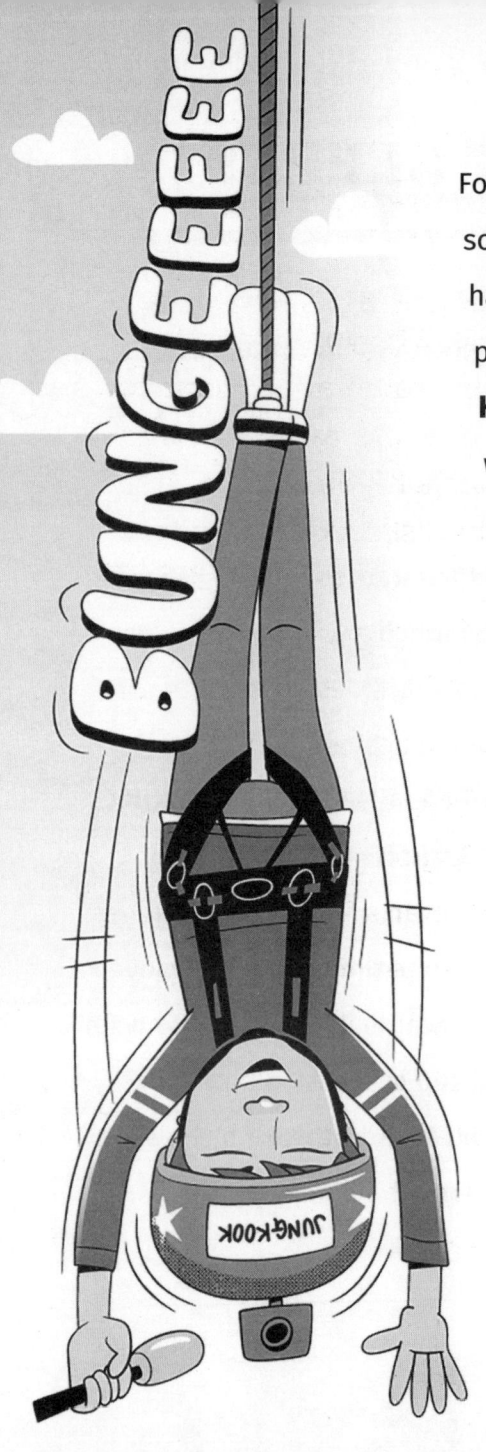

BUNGEEEEE

JUNG-KOOK

For lots of reasons, something seemed to have finally clicked into place for BTS. They were **HAPPIER** and surer of who they were, writing songs about the things that worried them *and* the things that brought them joy, blending upbeat pop and urban hip-hop to sound better and cooler than ever. And their dance routines were **OFF THE SCALE**.

FACT ALERT!

Around this time, BTS finally moved out of their one-bedroom apartment to a three-bedroom one. Jin and Suga were roommates, RM was with Jung Kook, and J-Hope, V and Jimin shared the biggest room. This moment is commemorated in the song 'Moving On'.

ARMY loved BTS's new direction. Actually, they *really, really* loved it! *The Most Beautiful Moment in Life Pt. 2* mini album not only became the fifth bestselling album in Korea in 2015 (despite only being released in November), but it also became BTS's first album to break the US Billboard 200 chart, at number 171. (Number 171 doesn't sound like a big deal, but it really was!) Things *finally* seemed to be going the way BTS wanted them to. **SO, WHAT NEXT?**

CHAPTER

5

THE GLOBAL BREAKTHROUGH

By the end of 2015, BTS were starting to get more famous around the world. The buzz about them was growing, and a huge part of that was due to their loyal ARMY spreading the word online. Things were starting to happen!

🔍 K-POP FOREVER

It was exciting, but the boys were also keen to stay true to their Korean heritage. They were proud to be a K-pop group and still sang in Korean, with a few English words and phrases. BTS honoured their culture wherever they could, incorporating Korean music and traditional dress into their modern style. So for now they concentrated their efforts for world domination closer to home with a tour of east and southeast Asia: **BTS LIVE THE MOST BEAUTIFUL MOMENT IN LIFE ON STAGE**.

 # FACT ALERT!

BTS have recorded Japanese versions of at least five of their albums because K-pop is super popular in Japan.

The tour included two nights at the Olympic Gymnastic Stadium in Seoul, South Korea's capital, in May 2016. At the time it was one of the largest venues in Korea, and performing there to over 25,000 fans was a **DREAM COME TRUE**. The boys found the experience really emotional and their genuine tears of joy and pride showed ARMY just how much it all meant to BTS.

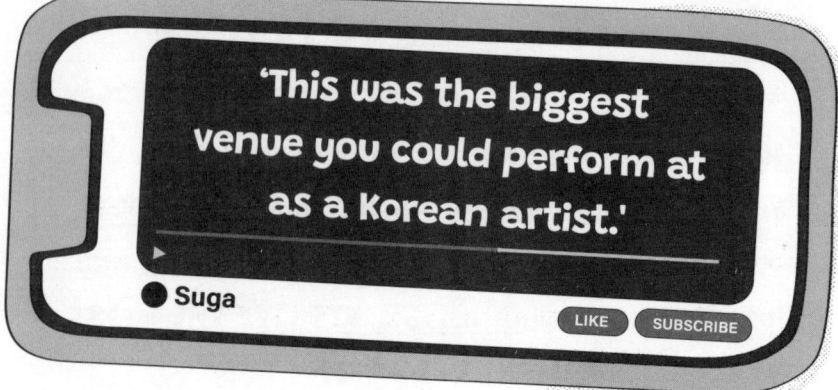

'This was the biggest venue you could perform at as a Korean artist.'

● Suga

LIKE   SUBSCRIBE

RISING STARS

In June 2016, BTS travelled further from home to perform at KCON in New York and LA.* The amazing

* KCON is an annual festival held in different locations around the world to promote K-pop and to give K-pop fans who don't live in Korea a chance to see their favourite idols perform.

response they got suggested that perhaps they might need to brush up on their English language skills . . .

FACT ALERT!

Over the years, BTS have also performed at KCONs in LA, Paris, Abu Dhabi and Mexico City.

After KCON, it was back home to finish their second full-length album, *Wings*. With its release in October 2016, things started to change for BTS in a **BIG** way.

WORLDWIDE SUCCESS

Wings sold more than **HALF A MILLION** copies in its first week in Korea, and the lead single, 'Blood, Sweat and Tears', finally gave BTS their first Korean number one. But that wasn't all: the song also went to number six on the **US BILLBOARD CHART!**

The dramatic and intense video
for 'Blood, Sweat and Tears' got a
staggering 6 million views in 24 hours, a
K-pop record at the time.

However, it wasn't just one mega-hit song that made
Wings so special – it also featured a solo track from
each member of BTS. Fans loved BTS as a group, but it
was also amazing to see their individual personalities
and styles. (Jimin's
song was the most
downloaded –
does that
mean he's the
most popular
member of BTS?
We certainly
couldn't pick a
favourite!)

There was even a special message to fans on the album too. The song '2! 3!' was dedicated to ARMY, with a message encouraging them to try and forget about any bad things and move forward to better days, together.

'We wanted to dedicate a song to our fans.'

RM

LIKE   SUBSCRIBE

🔍 I PURPLE YOU

Then, in November 2016, V uttered three iconic words that would change ARMY's life forever. At the end of a performance, he told fans, **'I PURPLE YOU'**. The rest of BTS had no idea what he meant, but ARMY understood. From then on, purple was BTS's signature colour, and fans often shared **PURPLE HEART EMOJIS** or used V's phrase to show their love for each other, and for BTS.

'Purple is the last colour of the rainbow. Purple means I will trust and love you for a long time . . . I just made it up!'

V

LIKE   SUBSCRIBE

So 2016 was a great year for BTS, and it was topped off when they won the prestigious **ASIAN MUSIC ARTIST OF THE YEAR** award. When they were training, the boys had watched the ceremony and imagined what it might be like to win an award, and now they'd done it. (They all cried when receiving the award, because it just meant so much to them. Adorable.) RM made sure to thank ARMY in his acceptance speech.

'We thank you all so much for believing in us to the end.'

RM

LIKE SUBSCRIBE

COULD LIFE GET ANY BETTER FOR **BTS?**

CHAPTER

6

DREAMING BIGGER

Yes, life could get better for BTS, and in 2017 some *truly amazing* things started to happen. (And we don't mean Jung Kook finally graduating high school, although that was very special!) After reaching **NUMBER ONE** and **WINNING ASIAN MUSIC ARTIST OF THE YEAR**, they had achieved everything that most K-pop stars dreamed of. But BTS felt like they were just getting started!

WORLD TOUR

Thanks to the power of social media, the internet and, of course, ARMY, more and more people around the world were talking about BTS. So they set off on their second world tour. **BTS LIVE TRILOGY EPISODE III: THE WINGS TOUR** was very different to their first world tour. Demand for tickets was high, and this time they were performing at **MUCH BIGGER** stadiums.

 # FACT ALERT!

Tickets for BTS's five US shows sold out **within minutes**.

The boys really enjoyed the tour too. As well as performing to their loyal fans, which always made them so happy, they also took breaks between shows and found time to relax and enjoy life. Of course, it was still **VERY** hard work, but being a K-pop star was starting to feel like **FUN** too.

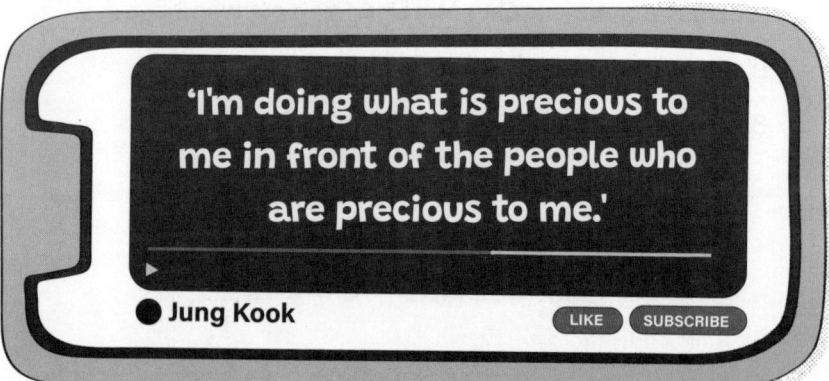

'I'm doing what is precious to me in front of the people who are precious to me.'

● Jung Kook

LIKE   SUBSCRIBE

Q USA BABY!

It was clear by now that BTS had a lot of fans in the USA, and they *demanded* to see more of their idols. So the group was invited to the famous US Billboard Music Awards in 2017. They were so nervous when they walked the red carpet, but no one could tell because they looked **SO COOL** in their slick black suits. (J-Hope's *iconic* silver boots were the standout fashion item that night.)

Q WINNERS

Every time BTS's name was even mentioned during the awards ceremony, the audience, which must have been 90% ARMY, *screamed!* When the group **WON** Top Social Artist, they went crazy. And they had every right to: this was **ALL DOWN TO ARMY**. It was based on the amount of fan interaction plus votes from fans, and BTS would go on to win it **FOUR MORE TIMES!**

'This award belongs to the people all around the world that shine the light and love on us by the millions and make BTS really proud.'

● RM

LIKE   SUBSCRIBE

FACT ALERT!

BTS beat Canadian pop star Justin Bieber to the Social Artist award. He had won it for the last six years in a row!

Winning an award in the USA felt amazing, and it seemed like it was just the start of their new journey. **(SPOILER ALERT: IT WAS!)** Lots of talented people were excited to meet BTS and keen to collaborate (make music) with them. It was so exciting, but a bit overwhelming too, especially as only RM was fluent in English and he often had to translate for the rest of the group.

FACT ALERT!

RM says that he learned English by watching the US TV show *Friends*.

BEYOND THE SCENE

With their popularity growing outside of Korea, loads of people kept asking what 'BTS' stood for. *You*, of course, know that it stands for Bangtan Sonyeondan or Bulletproof Boy Scouts, but it possibly sounded a bit niche to some people, so BTS decided to come up with something that worked better in English. They chose **'BEYOND THE SCENE'** to convey that BTS were bringing something new, something *extra* to the K-pop world. They also debuted a new door-inspired logo for BTS and ARMY.

It was a thoughtful move (and so typical of BTS), but all most fans *really* cared about was when the next album was coming out. Fortunately, they didn't have long to wait, as BTS launched their *Love Yourself* trilogy in September 2017. The mini album *Love Yourself: Her* went to number seven on the US Billboard album chart, while the lead single 'DNA' reached an impressive number sixty-seven on the Billboard Hot 100 singles chart. (The song is almost entirely in Korean, so most people who bought it wouldn't even know what BTS were singing about – they just knew that they liked it.)

Q | K-POP PIONEERS

It seemed that BTS were **UNSTOPPABLE**, and they were asked to appear on US chat shows (again with RM doing a lot of translating for the rest of the group). **IT WAS INCREDIBLE!**

'We became a
hot topic.'

▶ RM   [LIKE] [SUBSCRIBE]

But their proudest moment of 2017 came when they
became the first K-pop group EVER to perform at the
American Music Awards. Performing 'DNA' live was
an iconic moment, and not just for BTS. Everyone
watching (and there was a lot of ARMY in the audience,
as always) could see that they were **SUPERSTARS**.

Performing at the AMAs gave BTS a massive confidence
boost, and although they sometimes felt a bit out of
their depth in the USA (*everything* was so different),
they also felt like they were learning new skills.

A few days after the AMAs, BTS released a remix of 'Mic Drop' from *Love Yourself: Her* by DJ Steve Aoki with rapper Desiigner. It had an awesome video with a cool, anarchic theme (and typically **FIERCE DANCE MOVES**) and went to number twenty-eight in the Billboard Hot 100.

 **FACT ALERT!**

'Mic Drop' (remix) was the first of BTS's songs to be certified platinum in the USA (sell more than 1 million copies).

By the end of 2017, BTS were the most talked about group in the **WORLD** on X (formerly called Twitter). But there was so much more to come . . .

QUIZ: PART TWO

1

Which of BTS's videos was the first to get 100 million views on YouTube?

A 'DYNAMITE'

B 'DOPE'

C 'DNA'

2

Why did BTS travel to the USA in June 2016?

A TO GO TO DISNEYLAND

B TO PRACTISE THEIR ENGLISH

C TO PERFORM AT KCON

3 Which song gave BTS their first number one in Korea?

A 'BUTTER'

B 'BLOOD, SWEAT AND TEARS'

C 'BLACK SWAN'

4 Who said the famous words, 'I purple you'?

A V

B JIMIN

C J-HOPE

5 Who did BTS beat to win the 2017 US Billboard award for Top Social Artist?

A TAYLOR SWIFT

B ONE DIRECTION

C JUSTIN BIEBER

CHAPTER

7

WORLD DOMINATION

In 2018, things had never been better for BTS. Every album was moving higher up the charts, in so many different countries, and ARMY were busy spreading their love for BTS all around the world. However, no K-pop group had ever had a number one single or album in the USA, and BTS were determined to be the **FIRST**. It would be an amazing achievement for them, but also a proud moment for everyone in Korea.

🔍 BURN THE STAGE

Listening to their music wasn't enough, though – fans also wanted to know *everything* about BTS. Fortunately, the boys had that covered. As well as their regular YouTube series *(Run BTS)* they also released a behind-the-scenes eight-part documentary series (also on YouTube). *Burn the Stage* was filmed during **2017 BTS LIVE TRILOGY EPISODE III: THE WINGS TOUR**. It showed both the **HIGHS** and the **LOWS** of touring – how much the boys loved performing, but also the injuries and muscle strains that often occurred; the beautiful bond between the group and the stress of doing **SOOOOO** many interviews; the joy BTS brought to their fans as well as how unbelievably exhausted they were.

FACT ALERT!

Burn the Stage even had an appearance from V's adorable dog Yeontan, a black and tan Pomeranian, when he was just a tiny, fluffy puppy.

BTS finally scored their **FIRST NUMBER ONE** in the US charts in May 2018 with their album *Love Yourself: Tear*. It was an amazing moment not just for BTS but also for K-pop. In fact, the people of Korea were so proud of BTS's achievement that the country's president released a statement thanking them for **SPREADING JOY** to their country and across the world. They were also awarded special medals called the **ORDER OF CULTURAL MERIT** for promoting Korean culture around the world.

FACT ALERT!

BTS generate about $3.6 billion per year for South Korea's economy.

It was an amazing achievement and BTS felt honoured to be representing their country! The lead single, 'Fake Love', made it to number ten in the USA, and then just three months later they had **ANOTHER NUMBER ONE** album with *Love Yourself: Answer.*

ON TOUR

When BTS set off on their third world tour, **LOVE YOURSELF**, in August 2018, they were feeling on top of the world. And what a world they were living in! They still *felt* like the same people, but now they were travelling to concert venues in private jets and staying in fancy hotels, and they had security guards to protect them. The stadiums that they performed at were getting even bigger too!

'I felt like I'd become a world-class star.'

LIKE   SUBSCRIBE

● Jung Kook

On this tour, BTS also played shows in Europe for the first time, with their London dates selling out in record time. Demand for tickets was **SO HIGH** that they had to extend the tour by another **TWENTY SHOWS**. The extra dates were known as the **LOVE YOURSELF: SPEAK YOURSELF** tour. It was exhausting but amazing. In between shows, BTS rested their tired bodies (muscle injuries are part of pop-star life), gave TV interviews and tried to stay fit, healthy and motivated. They also had cameras following them the whole time and created another docuseries to show ARMY even more about their lives, called *Break the Silence*.

Wherever they went, BTS did things in incredible style. The first show of the extended tour, in California, lasted three hours and featured **FIREWORKS**, Jimin descending inside a **GIANT BUBBLE**, Jung Kook floating above the crowd and a sea of fans holding **GLOWING LIGHT STICKS** (that's something ARMYs do at every performance and it looks awesome).

 # FACT ALERT!

BTS were the first Korean artists to play at the famous Wembley Stadium in London. They were so proud to follow in the footsteps of music legends such as The Beatles, Adele and Beyoncé.

CHAPTER

8

ROLE MODELS

Although they were becoming more famous and more successful than they ever dreamed could be possible, BTS never forgot who it was all for – **THEIR FANS**. They truly cared about ARMY and appreciated their amazing support and all that it had done for them. When performing shows, they made sure to sing tracks from as many different albums as possible so fans would always hear their favourite songs. And they stayed connected to fans via social media as often as they could, wherever they were in the world.

'It's all thanks to our ARMY – I love you, ARMY!'

Jin

LIKE   SUBSCRIBE

BTS also never lost sight of one of the most important parts of their K-pop training: being **GOOD ROLE MODELS**. They tried their best to live their lives responsibly (no one is perfect, though, not even BTS) and to support their fans via their song lyrics. They wanted to share their feelings to show ARMY that they all felt the same things as them: the worries, the joy, the insecurities, the hopes and fears for the future.

FACT ALERT!

Jung Kook has the word 'ARMY' tattooed on the back of his hand.

PRIVATE LIVES

Although BTS share a lot with their fans, they rarely talk about their personal lives. They mention their families from time to time but are careful to keep the people they love out of the spotlight. Keeping some parts of their lives private is an important part of idol training, which is why BTS will never speak about their romantic partners. This is to protect people close to them from unwanted attention and also to make sure that the boys are recognised for their musical achievements, not who they might be dating!

🔍 MAKING A DIFFERENCE

In September 2018, BTS got the chance to take their message even further by delivering a powerful speech to the United Nations (UN) General Assembly in New York.* As part of a campaign to **EMPOWER YOUNG PEOPLE**, RM (with the rest of BTS standing proudly by his side) used his own experiences to encourage others to love themselves just as they are and to '**SPEAK YOURSELF**'.

---

* The UN is a global organisation in which representatives from different countries work together on issues that affect the whole world, such as poverty and war.

'Today I am who I am with all of my faults and my mistakes. Tomorrow I might be a tiny bit wiser and that would be me too. These faults and mistakes are what I am, making up the brightest stars in the constellation of my life. I have come to love myself for who I am, for who I was and for who I hope to become . . . I want to hear your voice; I want to hear your conviction. No matter where you're from, skin colour, gender identity, just speak yourself. Find your name, find your voice.'

IT WAS A REALLY PROUD, UNFORGETTABLE MOMENT FOR BTS.

CHAPTER

9

LIVING THE DREAM

Although BTS were global icons now, sometimes they still had to pinch themselves to check it was all really happening. One of those moments was at the 2019 Grammy Awards, when they were asked to **GIVE OUT AN AWARD**. (It was for Best R&B Album and H.E.R. won.) They were the first K-pop artists ever to present an award and it was so exciting. Afterwards they celebrated as much as if they had won and they became determined to **WIN** a Grammy Award one day. (They hadn't as of 2025, although they'd been nominated **FIVE TIMES** by this point, and we're sure they will one day!)

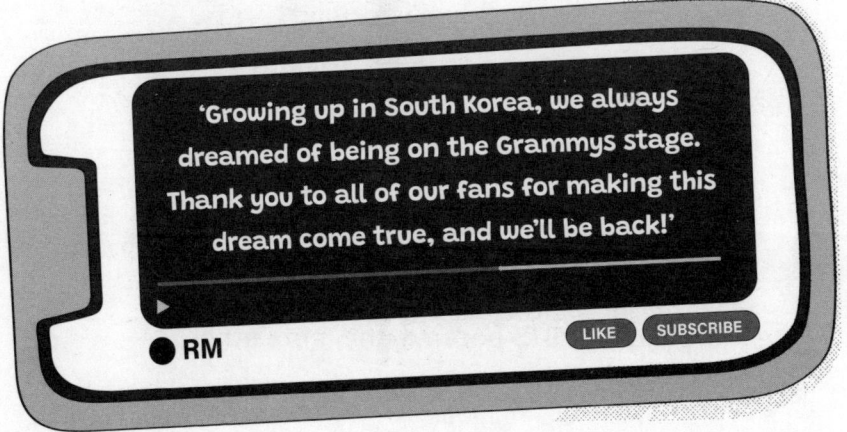

'Growing up in South Korea, we always dreamed of being on the Grammys stage. Thank you to all of our fans for making this dream come true, and we'll be back!'

RM

LIKE   SUBSCRIBE

BREAKING RECORDS

Amazingly, BTS also found time to release another mini album, *Map of the Soul: Persona*. It went straight to number one in the USA, making it their third album to top the charts within a year, a record rivalled only by The Beatles. It also went to number one in the UK and Australia and, at that time, was the bestselling album ever in South Korea.

 # FACT ALERT!

The song 'Make it Right' from *Map of the Soul: Persona* was co-written by the British pop star Ed Sheeran, along with RM, Suga and J-Hope.

 ## COLLABORATION

The more popular BTS became, the more other artists wanted to collaborate with them. Rapper and singer Nicki Minaj remixed their song 'Idol' from *Love*

Yourself: Answer, while singer Halsey featured on 'Boy with Luv' from *Map of the Soul: Persona*. The latter went to number eight in the US singles charts, as BTS crept ever closer to the sweet spot at the top of the chart.

Halsey was so impressed with BTS that she wrote an amazing article about them for the famous *Time* magazine, where they were named amongst the 100 Most Influential People of 2019. (They all counted as one entry, which meant that the list was really the **106** Most Influential People that year . . .)

 FACT ALERT!

On 21 May 2019, the iconic Empire State Building in New York City was lit up in purple for five minutes every hour from sunset to honour BTS and their fans.

Three more cool collaborations followed that year, including one for the soundtrack of their mobile game *BTS World.* The song, 'Dream Glow', featured Jin, Jimin and Jung Kook with Charli XCX. Another collab was the song 'A Brand New Day', starring J-Hope and V with Zara Larsson, and finally, 'All Night' was a rap song from RM and Suga with Juice WRLD.

FACT ALERT!

Toy company Mattel launched a range of BTS dolls inspired by the 'Idol' music video.

TIME FOR A REST

It was a busy time for BTS, and in August 2019, Big Hit Music announced that the boys would be taking their first break **SINCE 2013**. The announcement went down surprisingly well with ARMY, who mostly agreed

---

* Unfortunately the mobile game is no longer available.

that BTS probably did deserve a holiday. In fact, BTS only took a **MONTH** off (we imagine they slept for most of it) and many of them stayed active on social media the whole time so fans didn't have a chance to miss them too much.

 # FACT ALERT!

BTS UNIVERSE, the fictional storyline about an alternate universe version of BTS that was included in several of their music videos, became so popular that in 2019 they also launched a fifteen-episode 'webtoon' (digital comic) featuring versions of the boys in the fictional Korean town of Songju.

CHAPTER

10

RIDING HIGH

A refreshed BTS entered 2020 with BIG plans. First, they announced their **LARGEST EVER** world tour, due to begin in April.

Next, they launched **CONNECT, BTS**, an art project that spanned five cities across the world and twenty-two different artists. BTS had always understood the importance of connection, with each other and with their fans, and the artists' work aimed to explore the relationship between art, music and people. It was so cool and a totally unique thing to do.

One of the art pieces on display in Seoul, *Beyond the Scene* by Korean artist Yiyun Kang, showed BTS's dance moves projected as abstract shapes and silhouettes. Visitors could immerse themselves in the art piece and see how it made them feel. It must have felt very surreal when BTS themselves visited it!

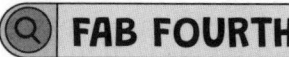

In February 2020, BTS broke even more records with the launch of their fourth full-length album, *Map of the Soul: 7*. It went straight to number one in the US Billboard chart. Again. It was BTS's **FOURTH** number one album in a row in the USA as well as being number one in Korea. However, they were still waiting for a **NUMBER ONE SINGLE...**

 **FACT ALERT!**

Map of the Soul: 7 was the bestselling album in the whole world in 2020 and the bestselling album of all time, as of 2024, in Korea.

It was also clear that BTS were getting more comfortable writing songs and singing in English. The lead single, 'ON', had more English language content than ever, with most of the chorus in English. The song's message to fans was to 'bring on the pain', which sounds, well, painful, but what they really meant

100

by it was to not be afraid to take risks and to just **GO FOR IT** in life, and in love.

In 2020 BTS finally performed at the Grammy Awards in the USA. It wasn't one of their own songs – they collaborated with rapper Lil Nas X on a version of his hit song 'Old Town Road'.

 **FACT ALERT!**

When BTS sang the chorus, they cleverly changed it to 'Seoul Town Road'.

After the Grammys, BTS continued rehearsing for their tour, which would be called **MAP OF THE SOUL**. They worked hard perfecting the choreography, choosing amazing costumes and making sure that it would be the best show they'd ever put on. They were all so excited, but then something unexpected happened which changed **EVERYTHING**.

QUIZ: PART THREE

1

Why did Korea's president thank BTS in May 2018?

A HE JUST LOVED THEIR MUSIC

B V FOUND HIS LOST DOG

C HE WAS SO PROUD OF THEIR FIRST US NUMBER ONE ALBUM

2

How many shows did BTS have to add to their Love Yourself tour because of the demand for tickets?

A TEN

B TWENTY

C THIRTY

3

Which British pop star co-wrote a song on *Map of the Soul: Persona*?

A ED SHEERAN

B STORMZY

C DUA LIPA

4

What was unusual about the lyrics for 'ON' from *Map of the Soul: 7*?

A THEY WERE WRITTEN BY JIN

B THEY FEATURED MORE ENGLISH THAN ANY OTHER PREVIOUS BTS SONG

C THEY WEREN'T CATCHY AT ALL

5

Who did BTS perform with at the 2020 Grammy Awards?

A LIL NAS X

B SNOOP DOGG

C MILEY CYRUS

CHAPTER 11

LOCKDOWN!

Since early 2020, news of a disease called Covid-19, or coronavirus, had been growing more worrying, and soon it became clear that it was a worldwide problem. Governments began to think about ways to slow down its spread, and the most obvious thing was to stop people gathering in large crowds and ask them to stay at home as much as possible, keeping their distance from other people. So that meant **NO MORE POP CONCERTS!** (It also meant no more school for a lot of people, which wasn't as fun as it sounded . . .)

BTS had to **POSTPONE** their tour, but they hoped it would only be for a short time. However, despite the world going into lockdown, coronavirus still developed into a global pandemic.* After a while, BTS had to cancel the tour completely. It was a massive blow, not just because the boys stood to lose around $200 million in ticket sales and merchandise, but because it meant they had nothing to do!

---

* A pandemic is when a disease or virus spreads quite quickly over a very large area, i.e. a country or the world.

Lockdown was pretty boring for a lot of people. (Some people, such as medical staff, supermarket workers and delivery drivers, still had to work, which wasn't easy but helped keep us safe and fed.) Staying home seemed fun at first (Jimin did loads of cleaning, Jin played video games, Suga worked on new music), but it soon got a bit hard to find things to do. BTS missed being pop stars, and they really missed their fans!

A lot of people were isolated from their family and friends during this period because of lockdown rules or because they lived far away. It was tough. BTS were lucky because they had each other to keep reminding themselves to **STAY POSITIVE** and **BE THANKFUL** (or to play video games against, try out new dance moves with or cook fancy food for). They also stayed connected to ARMY via social media and kept fans entertained with a compilation of concert videos they called **BANG BANG CON**.

'It felt like something was stolen from me. But despite all that, our fans kept tagging us and sending us messages. That's when I realised that they were always there for us.'

● Jimin

LIKE   SUBSCRIBE

But BTS really missed performing. So they decided to put on a concert that fans could watch **ONLINE**. Genius!

BANG BANG CON: THE LIVE

In June 2020, **756,000 FANS** from more than 100 different countries watched BTS perform an exclusive live concert called **BANG BANG CON: THE LIVE**.

ARMY was delighted to see their idols performing again and it meant that all BTS's practice (and costumes) for their cancelled tour didn't completely go to waste.

FACT ALERT!

Bang Bang Con: The Live also coincided with BTS's annual 'birthday' celebrations, **BTS Festa.**

HELPING ARMY

BTS were doing everything they could to help their beloved ARMY get through this difficult time. In September, they released a movie-length version of *Break the Silence* and put on two more online pay-per-view concerts in Seoul known as **MAP OF THE SOUL ON:E**. They were watched by **NEARLY 1 MILLION FANS!** It was quite a surreal experience for the boys, performing in an empty stadium with no live audience to look at or interact with. They had to work hard to generate the same energy and excitement that they felt during a live show. Fans just appeared as tiny video squares on a giant screen, and there was much less screaming than usual! However, BTS still spoke to fans directly and released hundreds of purple balloons in their honour. It was a tiny bit weird for everyone, but it was still *way* better than **NOT** performing at all.

'I wanted to show through this concert that we can still do something together.'

● RM

LIKE   SUBSCRIBE

Preparing for these virtual concerts gave BTS something to do when they really needed it and helped lots of their fans through a really difficult time. But BTS had been using their sudden spare time to work on new music too. And they were about to share something **SPECTACULAR!** Clue: It'll blow you away . . .

CHAPTER

12

LIGHTING IT UP

One *very* clever thing that BTS did during the coronavirus lockdown period was spend lots of time practising their English. With so much success in the US, the boys wanted to be able to express themselves more confidently and deeply in interviews. (And RM was getting a bit tired of translating all the time as well!)

FACT ALERT!

Most of BTS took English lessons, but Jimin claims that he just watched lots of shows in English on Netflix!

Q READY TO EXPLODE

Although BTS had achieved more than any other K-pop group and were proud of what they had done to promote their country, they finally felt ready to try something new – singing an entire song **IN ENGLISH**. The boys usually wrote their own songs, but they weren't quite ready to take on that challenge in English yet.

So they asked other songwriters to send them songs they thought might be a good fit and eventually chose the upbeat, catchy disco-pop song 'Dynamite'. It was the perfect pick-me-up for a world that was still suffering restrictions and hardships due to coronavirus, especially with the colourful, joyous video that accompanied it. (The boys just look like they're having so much **FUN!**)

'It was a song we made to simply enjoy with our fans.'

LIKE SUBSCRIBE

● Jin

🔍 TOP SPOT

When BTS released 'Dynamite' in August 2020, the world was a pretty upside-down place, so they had no idea how people would react. Amazingly it went

straight to number one on the US Billboard Hot 100 chart. **WOOO-HOOOOOOO!** They had finally done it! BTS were the first K-pop stars to have a number one single in the USA. It was an incredible moment in their career.

When BTS heard the news, they all cried and then celebrated, by themselves, with a cake. They dedicated their success, of course, to ARMY, who had made their dreams come true.

 # FACT ALERT!

'Dynamite' spent three weeks at number one and more than half a year in the Hot 100, a record for any K-pop song at the time.

There was no stopping BTS after this, and a second number one followed in October with the remix of 'Savage Love' by Jason Derulo. Attributed to BTS, it featured only Jung Kook's vocals (in English) and raps from Suga and J-Hope in Korean.

This was closely followed by a fifth US number one album in November, *BE*. There really was no stopping BTS, even when they couldn't actually go anywhere!

🔍 GRAMMYS GLORY?

With all their amazing success in the US, BTS hoped that they might finally get their first-ever Grammy Award nomination. They spent a tense evening waiting to find out: RM paced the room nervously, but V was busy thinking about whether he should go to the shop and buy a **GIMBAP** (a popular Korean seaweed rice roll). Jimin was focused on how badly he was doing in a game on his phone and J-Hope went to bed! Well, it was a **LOOOONG** wait while they announced the eighty-three different categories and nominees.

Fortunately BTS *were* nominated, in the Best Pop Duo/Group Performance category. (And, in case you were wondering, V actually got ramen noodles.) It was an honour just to be nominated and they were also asked to perform. They would have to wait **SEVERAL MONTHS** to find out if they'd actually won . . .

'I know the importance of the Grammys. It's a dream anyone working in music has.'

● Suga

LIKE   SUBSCRIBE

HAPPY BIRTHDAY, JIN

BTS's global popularity not only made everyone in Korea proud, it also brought extra visitors to the country and increased interest in **KOREAN CULTURE**. However, the law stated that all males had to have started military service by the time they were twenty-eight years old. Jin, the oldest member of BTS, was due to turn twenty-eight in December 2020! Unless the law changed, he would have to leave BTS to enlist in the army, just when things had started to go so well for them. It was **UNTHINKABLE**.

Fortunately, the Korean government agreed and changed the law so that cultural icons could **DELAY** their military service until they were **THIRTY YEARS OLD**. It was great news, at least for now . . .

CHAPTER

13

SMOOTH LIKE ....

In 2021, the coronavirus pandemic was still affecting the lives of many people. BTS were still not able to hold concerts for ARMY so they had to think of other ways to connect with them and help them get through an often-difficult time.

🔍 SO CLOSE

Some parts of pop-star life were getting back to normal, though, such as awards ceremonies, and it was time for BTS to find out if they had won a Grammy. Although the Grammys ceremony in 2021 was held without an audience, BTS contributed an amazing performance of 'Dynamite' (recorded in Korea). Despite the low-key ceremony, being nominated still felt like a really important moment for them. **WHAT IF THEY ACTUALLY WON?!!!!!** Suddenly life seemed as fresh and exciting as it had at the beginning of their pop career.

Sadly, the band didn't win (they were beaten by Lady Gaga and Ariana Grande's awesome song 'Rain on Me') but there was always next time. And being chosen to perform at the show with their first US number one single still felt pretty special, especially as they were the first K-pop group ever to perform at the Grammys.

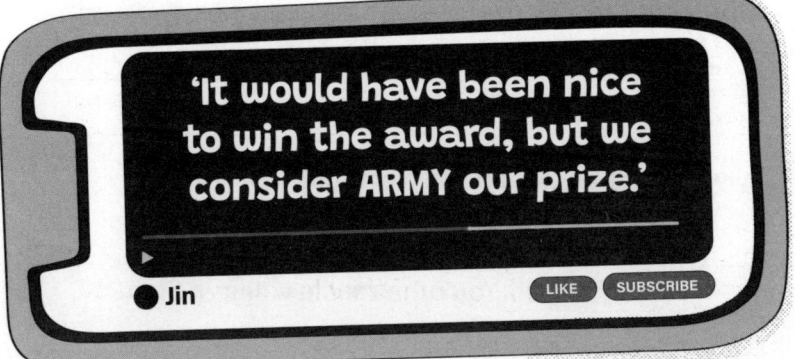

'It would have been nice to win the award, but we consider ARMY our prize.'

▶ ● Jin   LIKE   SUBSCRIBE

Q SPREADING THE LOVE

After the success of 'Dynamite', BTS were keen to write their own song in English, but it wasn't so easy. (Writing a good pop song is hard enough in your own language, let alone in a **SECOND LANGUAGE!**) When they found the song 'Butter', it seemed perfect for them, apart from the raps. So RM rewrote the raps to fit their style and earned a songwriting credit on 'Butter'.

'Butter' was number one for an incredible **TEN** weeks in the USA, but the music video was even more record breaking (and not because of Jung Kook's scene-stealing, fabulous purple hair). It even broke **FOUR** Guinness World Records on YouTube as soon as it was released:

- ♪ Most views for the premiere of any type of video on YouTube
- ♪ Most viewers for the premiere of a music video on YouTube
- ♪ Most viewed YouTube music video in twenty-four hours
- ♪ Most viewed YouTube music video in twenty-four hours by a K-pop group

 FACT ALERT!

BTS have held more than twenty-three Guinness World Records, including fastest to reach **1 million followers** on Tik Tok. (It took ARMY just three hours and thirty-one minutes to reach that total.)*

---

* Many of these records have since been broken.

PERMISSION TO DANCE

There seemed to be no stopping BTS. Their next single, 'Permission to Dance', their third in English, went straight to the top of the US Billboard chart, replacing **THEIR OWN SONG** 'Butter'!

As the world tried to get back to normal after the global pandemic, 'Permission to Dance' seemed to be exactly what people needed to hear. The song's message was simple: you don't need anyone's permission to dance, so just go and do it! **HAVE FUN.** The video had a cool, cowboy vibe and featured a symbolic purple (of course) balloon floating through the sky.

 # FACT ALERT!

'Permission to Dance' was co-written by Ed Sheeran and does not feature any raps. BTS's main rappers, RM, Suga and J-Hope, all sing instead.

BTS followed up the single with a mini world tour with the same name. **PERMISSION TO DANCE ON STAGE** included twelve shows in North America and South Korea, which were the boys' first in-person concerts in two years. **THEY COULDN'T WAIT!**

(Q) BACK IN BUSINESS

Travelling around again felt a little weird after so long, and the boys worried that they had lost some of the fitness and stamina they needed to perform, but they were so excited to see ARMY in person again. Nothing could come close to the joy they felt when sharing special moments with their fans.

Even rehearsing for the tour felt wonderful, and they were determined that everything would be **PERFECT** for their fans. So they practised hard, even hitting the gym after rehearsals to make sure they were in the best physical condition.

'We worked really hard to perfect everything for this.'

When BTS saw the sea of lights waving at them
and heard the screams of joy at the first US show,
they knew that it had all been worth it. The nerves
disappeared, and they felt so happy to be back on
stage where they belonged. In the past, touring had
felt exhausting and repetitive at times, but now it felt
fresh and exciting. It was **FUN** and it was a close call
between who enjoyed it the most – BTS or ARMY.

CHAPTER

14

OUT OF THIS WORLD

BTS finished 2021 on a high, with a sixth US number one single in just over a **YEAR**. It was a collaboration, 'My Universe', with British group Coldplay. Everyone loved BTS and wanted to work with them!

Their cool style and love of fashion had also been recognised by the famous fashion brand Louis Vuitton, who had made them brand ambassadors. (This basically means they got some amazing clothes for free!) They also decided it was time to stop living together and moved into their own luxury apartments in Seoul, each costing several million dollars! They had certainly come a long way from seven bunk beds in a one-bedroom apartment!

 # FACT ALERT!

Jin and RM are neighbours, living in the same super-expensive apartment complex.

But most incredible of all, they won **THREE** American Music Awards: Artist of the Year (the biggest award of the night), Best Pop Group and Best Pop Song for 'Butter'. It was a fantastic achievement for BTS (we actually think they should have won even **MORE** awards though) and another first for K-pop. It was extra-special for BTS as the AMAs had been where they'd given their first ever live performance in the US, in 2017. Back then they could never have dreamed of being the stars of the show, and as usual they dedicated their success to ARMY.

'We purple you!'

GIVING BACK

Things were going unbelievably well for BTS, but they knew that not everyone was as lucky as they were. They appreciated everything they had and were determined to use their fame and popularity to help others. Ever since RM's speech to the UN back in 2018, the group had been working with UNICEF (United Nations Children's Fund) on the **LOVE MYSELF** campaign. Its aim was to end abuse and bullying, and to increase self-esteem and wellbeing for children and young people all around the world. By the end of 2021, BTS had helped to raise $3.6 million for the campaign and are still involved with it today.

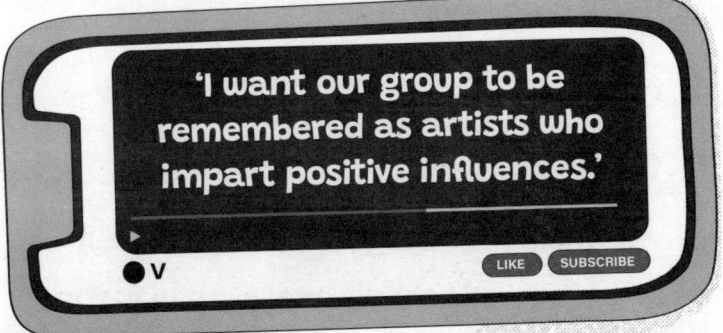

'I want our group to be remembered as artists who impart positive influences.'

● V   LIKE   SUBSCRIBE

WHAT NEXT?

With extra confidence, thanks to their amazing win at the AMAs, BTS wanted to do even more amazing things in 2022. They had achieved so much already but it was time to think long and hard about what they *all* wanted to do next. With seven members, any individual's decision would affect the whole group. What if someone decided that they didn't want to be in BTS any more? **(WHAT?!!!! DON'T EVEN GO THERE ...)**

🔍 BACK HOME

While BTS thought about big, life-changing questions, they were overjoyed to finally be allowed to perform in Korea for the first time in more than two years. However, it was a bittersweet experience as due to Covid restrictions, Korean fans weren't allowed to stand up, sing or cheer!

'The thing is, especially in Korea, I usually get to hear the fans chant and sing with me. I didn't get to hear that today though. And that made it really difficult for me.'

● Jung Kook

LIKE SUBSCRIBE

🔍 LOOKING BACK

The group also put together an anthology album featuring their favourite hits from all their different albums. Titled *Proof*, it meant that newer ARMY members who hadn't been following BTS since their debut could discover some of their earlier hits.

Despite being more than **TWO HOURS LONG**, it went straight to number one in the US Billboard album chart (BTS's sixth number one album in a row – WOW). The album also featured some new songs, including the lead single 'Yet to Come (The Most Beautiful

Moment)'. Its message seemed hopeful that BTS saw their future together, and the accompanying music video set in the desert referenced a lot of their earlier videos too.

 **FACT ALERT!**

'Yet to Come (The Most Beautiful Moment)' was BTS's first single in Korean for two years.

However, just **DAYS** later, BTS made an announcement that fans had been hoping would *never* come . . .

QUIZ: PART FOUR

1

What was unique about BTS's Map of the Soul tour in 2020?

A THEY PLAYED IN ANTARCTICA

B V'S DOG PERFORMED WITH THEM

C IT WAS CANCELLED DUE TO COVID-19

2

How does Jimin claim that he learned English?

A FROM ED SHEERAN

B FROM NETFLIX

C FROM READING HARRY POTTER

3 How long did 'Dynamite' spend at number one in the US?

A ONE WEEK

B TWO WEEKS

C THREE WEEKS

4 Which member of BTS has a songwriting credit on 'Butter'?

A RM

B SUGA

C JUNG KOOK

5 How many American Music Awards did BTS win in 2021?

A ONE

B TWO

C THREE

CHAPTER

15

BIG NEWS

Ever since their one-year anniversary of the band in June 2014, BTS has held BTS Festa to celebrate the anniversary of their debut with fans. It was a time to **GIVE SOMETHING BACK** to their fans via exclusive videos and other content, and also a chance to reflect on and appreciate everything they had achieved so far. **EVERYONE LOOKED FORWARD TO IT.**

BTS FESTA 2022

By the time BTS Festa 2022 came around, the group were more successful than they could ever have imagined.

- They had hit singles and albums all around the world.
- They were the leaders of a global K-pop music revolution.
- They brought joy and comfort to their dedicated ARMY of fans.
- They used their fame to help others who needed it.

FACT ALERT!

By now, each member of BTS had a
personal fortune of more than $20 million.

However, they had been working incredibly hard for
more than **TEN YEARS** (including K-pop training too)
with only a couple of short breaks. They had been
teenagers when they started out and now they were
grown adults. They had spent so much time together,
and it had been truly amazing, but now they needed
SPACE. They all felt that they should take time to work
out who they were as individuals before they could
decide how they wanted BTS to progress in the future.

'It's time to close
this book and open a
new one.'

▶
● Suga   LIKE   SUBSCRIBE

So, the boys had made their decision – it was time to scale back BTS (for now) and focus on **SOLO PROJECTS**. They all agreed, but then it was time to let ARMY know. How would they react? RM worried that ARMY would be disappointed and upset, but Jung Kook felt that ARMY would want to grow with them and still follow their solo music. Whatever happened, BTS agreed that ARMY should be the first to know about their big news.

Q THE REAL BTS DINNER PARTY

BTS wanted ARMY to hear the news directly from them so, as part of BTS Festa, they held The Real BTS Dinner Party (streamed on YouTube). Surrounded by purple balloons, the boys tucked into a huge feast and chatted about what was happening in their lives now and reminisced about the past, just like best friends do.

FACT ALERT!

BTS's feast included most of their favourite foods, such as ramen noodles, pizza, sushi, crab, shrimp, meat skewers and a cheese and fruit platter.

When the conversation turned to what BTS had planned for the future, the boys were able to explain exactly why they needed to **TAKE A BREAK**. Everyone took turns to speak, telling ARMY how they truly felt.

RM explained how being leader of the group and the spokesperson felt like a lot of responsibility sometimes, while Suga revealed that he wanted to experiment with creating different types of music and also learn to dance better. Jin said that he planned to play a **LOT** of video games for a bit, while Jung Kook wanted to learn lots of new things and have some fun. J-Hope was already planning his solo music and said that it felt like this was BTS's 'second chapter'. V was looking forward to showing people a different side to him, while Jimin was also writing songs and preparing music.

'Do whatever feels right for you.'

RM

LIKE   SUBSCRIBE

The boys were so worried about how ARMY would feel and many fans *were* extremely upset (the boys cried a lot too, especially J-Hope!). However, after watching the video, most of ARMY appreciated BTS's reasons and just wanted them to be **HAPPY**. Taking breaks is a fairly common thing for K-pop groups to do, so they believed BTS when they promised to come back.

 # FACT ALERT!

Not everyone was happy, though. The value of BTS's management company plummeted by 28% after their announcement, losing $1.7 billion in just one hour . . .

CHAPTER

16

BEYOND BTS

Telling ARMY they planned to take a break was a **MASSIVE RELIEF** to BTS – now they could get on with making their individual plans happen! It wasn't just J-Hope and Jimin who had plans for solo music. Every member of BTS was keen to try **SOMETHING NEW**, and they'd all worked on their own music alongside BTS over the years, often releasing snippets called 'mixtapes' or collaborating on other artists' music. Now, though, it was a chance to really explore *what* they wanted to say and *how* they wanted to say it. It was exciting, but also a tiny bit scary going solo. What if no one liked their music? **(AS IF THAT WOULD *EVER* HAPPEN!)**

FACT ALERT!

BTS all got the number seven tattooed on various parts of their bodies, in honour of their group and also to stay connected while they were apart.

SOLO SUCCESS

Jung Kook was the first to go it alone when he featured on US singer Charlie Puth's break-up song 'Left and Right' in June 2022, which reached number twenty-two in the US Billboard chart. Jung Kook also featured in the soundtrack for the 2022 FIFA World Cup with the uplifting song 'Dreamers', and he performed it at the opening ceremony in Qatar.

Next was J-Hope's album *Jack-in-the-Box*. J-Hope had released a couple of singles before his album, including the insanely catchy **'CHICKEN NOODLE SOUP'**, featuring US singer Becky G, in 2019. (Check out the video on YouTube and see if you can do the crazy dance that goes with the song!) *Jack-in-the-Box* went to number six in the US Billboard album chart and number two in South Korea. J-Hope also performed at the famous US music festival Lollapalooza. A few months later, he also released *In the Box* on Disney+, a documentary about making his album.

For his album, J-Hope was inspired by his own life, and RM took a similar approach with his solo album *Indigo*, which referenced personal stories and moments.

 **FACT ALERT!**

Indigo peaked at number three in the US Billboard album chart, the highest for a solo Korean artist in history at the time.

Jin took a different approach, just releasing one dreamy song, 'The Astronaut'. Co-written with BTS's old friends Coldplay, it topped streaming charts in **104 COUNTRIES** and made it to number 51 on the US Billboard Hot 100.

And working on solo music didn't mean that the boys couldn't collaborate, if the right song came along. Credited as BTS, Jin, Jimin, V and Jung Kook all sang on Benny Blanco's 'Bad Decisions', featuring rapper Snoop Dogg. The funny music video showed a BTS superfan

(Blanco) preparing for a BTS concert, making a poster, practising his dance moves and baking a special purple cake, only to learn that he was a whole day early for the show!

Just like BTS, the boys' solo music was a hit all around the world. **EVERYONE LOVED IT.**

'The most important thing is that music truly transcends languages, nationalities and races.'

RM

LIKE   SUBSCRIBE

🔍 DUTY CALLS

In October 2022, BTS performed together for the final time before their break, in J-Hope, Jung Kook and

Jimin's home city of Busan. Once again, fans were not allowed to sing along, cheer or even stand up, although they couldn't help but let out a small scream when BTS first entered the stage. **(WHO COULD BLAME THEM FOR THAT?)**

If fans had secretly hoped that BTS might change their minds about their break, in December 2022 they realised that was never going to happen. Jin, the eldest member, enlisted for his military service just after his thirtieth birthday. (Remember that law we told you about earlier?) He would be gone for at least eighteen months. It was only a matter of time before the rest of the group would have to enlist. The rest of BTS and ARMY were sad to see Jin go, but incredibly **PROUD** of him too.

 # FACT ALERT!

Jin had to shave off his wonderful hair to comply with the army's rules. Of course he still looked 'worldwide handsome'!

However, there was a ray of hope: K-pop stars are still allowed to take part in events that benefit their country during their national service. BTS would still be able to do *some* music-related activities and keep releasing the solo music and TV shows that they'd been working on. **YAY!**

NEXT UP

The fifth member of BTS to release his solo music was Jimin. He had found it strange working alone at first, but his BTS brothers helped him to find his voice. For his album *Face*, he looked back on the challenges he

faced during the Covid lockdown period, feelings of loneliness and self-doubt. He hoped that fans would relate to these feelings and see the real Jimin behind his glamorous pop star image.

'I want to be better and cooler.'

● Jimin

LIKE SUBSCRIBE

FACT ALERT!

The lead single on Jimin's album, 'Like Crazy', went straight to number one in the US Hot 100, making Jimin not only the first member of BTS to have a solo chart topper, but also the first solo artist from Korea to do so.

Soon, J-Hope became the second member of BTS to enlist in the military, followed by Suga, but not before releasing his own album, *D-Day.* Suga did things a little differently, though, using another alias, Agust D, for his solo music. (It must be confusing for his friends, though: do they call him Yoon-gi, Suga or Agust D?)

Suga is often called the **HARDEST WORKING MEMBER** of BTS. He somehow finds time to make his own music, produce for other people, take English lessons, work on his dancing *and* do Pilates every day to stay strong.

Suga also became the first member of BTS to tour with his solo music, performing twenty-eight shows in North America and Asia before enlisting. Like J-Hope, he also released a documentary about making his album, called *Suga: Road to D-Day*.

---

* Due to an old shoulder injury, Suga cannot perform active duties, so he has been serving in the public sector instead.

Jung Kook was next to release a solo album, *Golden*. Although the title was a cute nod to his status in BTS as the golden maknae (youngest), the album was all about showing that he was grown up. It was also sung in English and featured co-writing credits from other stars, such as Ed Sheeran and Shawn Mendes.

Jung Kook later released a movie-length documentary called *I Am Still*, about making this album.

🔍 LAST BUT NOT LEAST

V took a little longer than the rest of BTS to perfect his solo music, but it was worth the wait. While the others had chosen a modern pop, rap or R&B style, V went for something a little more **OLD SCHOOL**, with jazz and classic R&B on his album *Layover*. However, V kept it totally modern too, with the 'ping' of text messages in his video for the lead single, 'Rainy Days'. (His adorable dog **YEONTAN** also starred in the video, and on the album cover too.)

CHAPTER

17

YET TO COME

In December 2023, RM, Jimin, V and Jung Kook all enlisted for their military service. Jimin and Jung Kook actually enlisted together, as part of the 'military companion' programme in which friends are allowed to stay **TOGETHER**. It's so nice to think of them being able to support each other during their service and share the experience.

FACT ALERT!

Jimin and Jung Kook's amazing friendship can also be seen in the hilarious and adorable documentary series *Are You Sure?!*, in which the boys go on summer adventures together in New York, Jeju Island, South Korea and Sapporo in Japan. (V also appears at some points too!)

🔍 KEEPING ARMY HAPPY

Although BTS have been out of the spotlight in the last couple of years (at least compared to the height of their success when they were **EVERYWHERE**), it

really hasn't been as bad as many fans feared. The documentary *BTS Monuments: Beyond the Star* showed the boys reflecting on their whole career, sharing their highs and lows and some really personal feelings about their journey. It was a **MUST-WATCH** for any BTS fan who needed to be reminded how amazing they are, how incredible their success has been, and also how much they care about ARMY.

 # FACT ALERT!

In 2023, LEGO® released a cute BTS set, themed around the group's 'Dynamite' video. In one store it sold out within 145 minutes!

For fans who wanted something a little different, *Begins ≠ Youth* was a fictional recreation of BTS's alternate universe story, with actors playing fictionalised versions of the boys. **CONFUSING? BRILLIANT?** Maybe both . . .

NON-STOP MUSIC

In 2024, despite all serving in the military, every member of BTS released new music and content. J-Hope released a documentary on Amazon Prime about his dance journey, called *Hope on the Street*, with an accompanying soundtrack album. RM also released his second album, *Right Place, Wrong Person*, plus a cool collaboration with Megan Thee Stallion called 'Neva Play'.

Meanwhile, Jimin also released a second album, *Muse*, which included the incredibly catchy song 'Who', about being in love with someone he had never met. V's single 'Fri(end)s' was about falling for a friend, while Jung Kook's 'Never Let Go' was about holding on to love. The video featured footage of ARMY supporting BTS, as if Jung Kook was reassuring everyone that he had not forgotten them. **AWWW!**

So thanks to solo music, documentaries, social media and even a few group appearances, ARMY have had *just* about enough BTS to keep them going. (We still find it amazing that BTS have managed to be pop stars and fulfil their military service!) But life isn't the same without BTS making new albums, touring or just generally making the world seem like a better place.

🔍 NOT LONG NOW

However, Jin and J-Hope have already completed their military service. As they return to civilian life (and reconnect with fans, yay), the prospect of BTS getting back together is getting tantalisingly close. When Jin released his perfectly titled album *Happy* in November 2024, it meant that every member of the group had released a solo album. It sounded amazing, of course, but NOTHING is as incredible as RM, Jin, Suga, J-Hope, Jimin, V and Jung Kook making music together. We just cannot wait to hear the kind of music they will create when BTS reunite in 2025. We know that it will be **EPIC!**

CHAPTER

18

BE LIKE BTS

BTS have always wanted their music and their stories to support and inspire others, especially ARMY. They know that life is a journey and they hope that they can help people along the way. Here's what we've learned from BTS:

Love yourself – you're not perfect, no one is. Just be kind to yourself, especially when you mess up.

Friendship is everything – with good friends by your side, you will be stronger and have way more fun.

Be genuine – don't try and act like someone else because you think people might like you more. You're great as you are.

Work hard – achieving your dreams won't happen overnight, it will take hard work and dedication. You can do it!

Support others – be a good friend and use your voice to help others who need it.

You can always level up – keep trying different things and learning new skills.

Join together to make things happen – just like ARMY did to make BTS global superstars!

Stay positive – even when times feel tough, remember that things will get better.

Q ANSWERS

Q Part One:

1) C   4) C

2) B   5) C

3) A

Q Part Two:

1) B   4) A

2) C   5) C

3) B

Q Part Three:

1) C   4) B

2) B   5) A

3) A

Q Part Four:

1) C   4) A

2) B   5) C

3) C

SOURCES

Introduction
Quote 1: https://www.usmagazine.com/celebrity-news/news/did-bts-break-up-why-the-band-is-taking-a-hiatus-after-9-years/
Quote 2: https://www.today.com/popculture/music/bts-military-service-rcna128237

Chapter 2
Quote 1: BTS Ultimate Fanbook (Future PLC, 2023), page 39.
Quote 2: BTS Ultimate Fanbook (Future PLC, 2023), page 30.
Quote 3: K-Pop Kings (Buster books, 2021), page 54.
Quote 4: https://www.youtube.com/watch?v=5vXiaaIxPHs

Chapter 3
Quote 1: https://www.papermag.com/break-the-internet-bts#rebelltitem67
Quote 2: BTS Ultimate Fanbook (Future PLC, 2023), page 14.
Quote 3: 'The Beginning'. BTS Monuments: Beyond the Star. Disney+, 20 December 2023.

Chapter 4
Quote 1: 'The Beginning'. BTS Monuments: Beyond the Star. Disney+, 20 December 2023.
Quote 2: 'The Beginning'. BTS Monuments: Beyond the Star. Disney+, 20 December 2023.

Chapter 5
Quote 1: 'The Beginning'. BTS Monuments: Beyond the Star. Disney+, 20 December 2023.
Quote 2: 'Adolescence'. BTS Monuments: Beyond the Star. Disney+, 20 December 2023.
Quote 3: https://www.newsweek.com/bts-kim-taehyung-purple-meaning-1453501
Quote 4: 'Adolescence'. BTS Monuments: Beyond the Star. Disney+, 20 December 2023.

Chapter 6
Quote 1: 'The Beginning'. BTS Monuments: Beyond the Star. Disney+, 20 December 2023.
Quote 2: https://www.youtube.com/watch?v=kIKPZTZC4fI
Quote 3: 'Adolescence'. BTS Monuments: Beyond the Star. Disney+, 20 December 2023.

Chapter 7
Quote 1: 'Pursuit of Happiness'. BTS Monuments: Beyond the Star. Disney+, 27 December 2023.

Chapter 8
Quote 1: https://www.youtube.com/watch?v=gIbwq2keLks
Quote 2: https://www.forbes.com/sites/caitlinkelley/2018/09/25/bts-deliver-speech-at-united-nations-urging-young-people-to-find-your-voice/

Chapter 9
Quote 1: https://variety.com/2019/music/news/bts-grammys-present-awards-kpop-1203130948/

Chapter 11
Quote 1: 'Disconnected'. BTS Monuments: Beyond the Star. Disney+, 27 December 2023.
Quote 2: 'Disconnected'. BTS Monuments: Beyond the Star. Disney+, 27 December 2023.

Chapter 12
Quote 1: 'Disconnected'. BTS Monuments: Beyond the Star. Disney+, 27 December 2023.
Quote 2: https://www.teenvogue.com/story/bts-reaction-2021-grammy-nomination

Chapter 13
Quote 1: 'Disconnected'. BTS Monuments: Beyond the Star. Disney+, 27 December 2023.
Quote 2: 'Welcome!'. BTS Monuments: Beyond the Star. Disney+, 3 January 2024.

Chapter 14
Quote 1: https://www.youtube.com/watch?v=PTfPWxjgjoM
Quote 2: 'Welcome!'. BTS Monuments: Beyond the Star. Disney+, 3 January 2024.
Quote 3: https://metro.co.uk/2022/03/11/bts-star-jungkook-admits-he-struggled-to-perform-for-silent-crowd-16260064/

Chapter 15
Quote 1: 'Begin and Again'. BTS Monuments: Beyond the Star. Disney+, 3 January 2024.
Quote 2: https://www.youtube.com/watch?v=1t0iJ7F_k9Q

Chapter 16
Quote 1: 'The Beginning'. BTS Monuments: Beyond the Star. Disney+, 20 December 2023.
Quote 2: https://www.vulture.com/article/bts-solo-projects-tv-shows-group-activities.html

Look out for more of your favourites in
THE
WORLD of
series

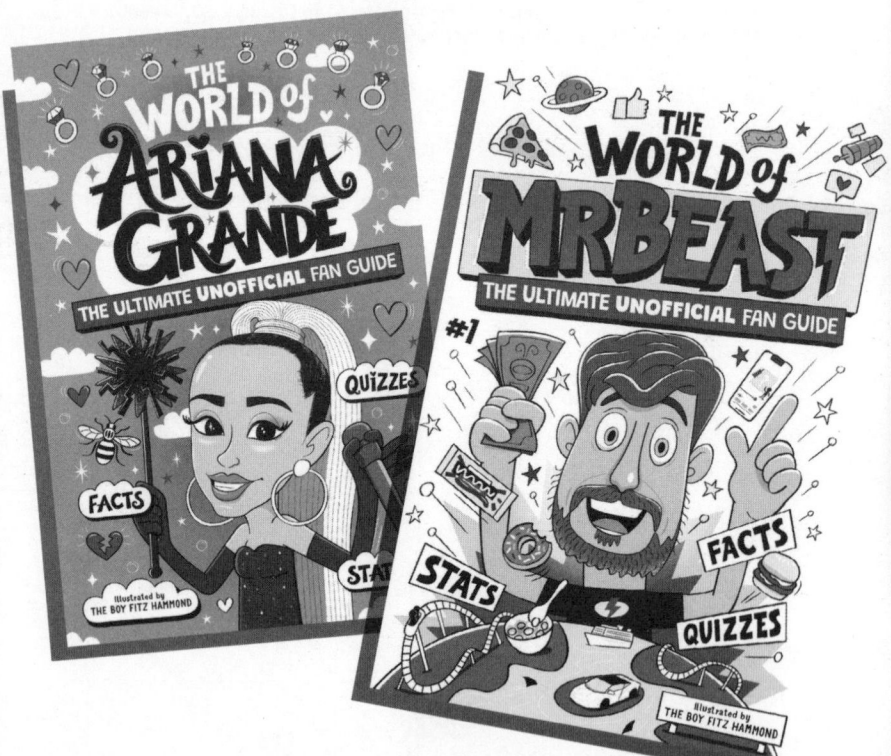